Dedication

To my beloved wife, Portia Osei-Owusu, your unwavering love, strength, and wisdom have been my anchor.

To my children, Ezekiel, Eliana, and Emersyn, may you always walk boldly in your God-given purpose.

And to every anointed and gifted minister who has ever felt unseen, misunderstood, or frustrated, this book is for you. May it remind you that your calling is not in vain and your labor is not forgotten.

Acknowledgment

I extend my deepest gratitude to my National Head of the Church of Pentecost U.S.A Inc. Apostle Seth Asante, My Regional Head Rev. Frank Agyemang Prempeh, To the National Executive Council and to everyone who played a part in bringing this book to life. To Rev. Nana Yeboah and to Rev. Emmanuel Agormeda thank you for being a help and support throughout my life. Dr. Kwame Boateng thank you for writing the forward for this book and thanks for the mentorship and love.

To my incredible editing team, Lindsay and Georgina, thank you for your careful eyes, thoughtful feedback, and commitment to excellence. You labored over every word and helped shape this message with clarity and grace.

To Wiggles, thank you for capturing the heart of this work through your creative design.

To Emmanuel, your skillful formatting brought structure and polish to these pages, and I'm truly grateful.

To my Wife Portia Osei-Owusu, thank you for the spiritual and morale support.

This project would not have been possible without each of you. Thank you for believing in the vision.

table of contents

Chapter

01.

Chapter

02.

Chapter

03.

Foreword

There comes a moment in every generation when the call of God must be answered—not in isolation, but in unity. Anointed But Accountable is that clarion call. It is a prophetic and practical guide for ministers, both upcoming and seasoned, urging us to rise above division and walk together in love, purpose, power of the Spirit, and accountability.

Pastor Yaw Osei Owusu has penned more than a book—he has released a mantle. With deep spiritual insight and the authority of lived experience, he challenges us to embrace the sacred tension between anointing and responsibility. He reminds us that the oil of God flows most freely where humility, honor, and accountability are present.

This book serves as a bridge—linking generations, healing misunderstandings, and igniting a shared passion for advancing the Kingdom. Whether you are just discovering your calling or have walked in it for decades, Anointed But Accountable will stir your spirit, sharpen your focus, and strengthen your resolve.

As Jesus declared in John 8:29: "The one who sent me is with me; he has not left me alone, for I always do what pleases him." Let these pages awaken a deeper commitment in you—not just to be anointed, but to be accountable and relevant. For in that balance lies the true power of ministry that transforms lives and glorifies God.

Dr. Kwame Boateng
(Senior Pastor of Shepherd's House Worship Center)

Introduction

Ministry is a calling, a divine assignment wrapped in purpose and passion. But what happens when your calling finds itself intertwined with someone else's vision? What happens when your ministry exists within a ministry, a para-church organization thriving under the covering of a local church? This is the tension, the beauty, and the challenge that countless ministers face.

In 2009, while pursuing my studies at Liberty University and serving as the Student President of PENSA (Pentecost Students and Associates) in the Church of Pentecost Richmond District, God placed a unique burden on my heart. It was a call to create a ministry that could operate alongside the local church, a para-church organization designed to address unmet needs within the church. This calling led to the birth of True Worshippers Inc., a ministry that has now thrived for over 15 years.

God's vision for True Worshippers was clear from the start: examine what is missing within the local church and find ways to maximize on those areas for His glory. As I sought God's guidance, one glaring gap became apparent. It wasn't due to neglect or lack of effort by the church but rather the inevitable constraints of time and structure. That gap was extended, uninhibited praise and worship, a dedicated time and space for believers to come together and worship God without the typical constraints of a Sunday service.

With this revelation, I made a promise to God. I told Him that True Worshippers would be a ministry dedicated to gathering people from different churches across the DMV (D.C., Maryland, and Virginia) area to worship and praise Him, all night, under one roof. This vision filled me with excitement and conviction. I began sharing the idea with friends from different churches, inviting them to join me in this divine assignment. One of the first people who embraced this vision wholeheartedly was Theo B. Darko, who at the time was a member of The Apostolic Church and now serves at Redeemer's Church. Together, we rallied other friends and partners to help organize our first event, which took place on July 4th, 2009: "A Night of True Praise & Worship."

That night was nothing short of extraordinary. We featured renowned gospel artists Sonnie Badu and Kenneth Appiah and were astonished when 350 people showed up for our first event. It was a testament to God's hand on this ministry. However, as exciting as that night was, it revealed an immature perspective we held at the time. The event's name, "A Night of True Praise & Worship," carried an unintended implication that what happened during regular church services wasn't "real" worship. While we were sincere in our intentions, this mindset was misguided, and it's something I'll delve deeper into as we progress through this book.

As True Worshippers grew, so did the challenges. What I had not anticipated were the fights, misunderstandings, and insecurities that would arise both in me and among others. I was young and immature, lacking the experience needed to navigate the complexities of leading a para-church ministry while being deeply involved in my local church. Many within my church, and others, struggled to understand what we were doing and why. This often led to tensions and questions about the ministry's intentions, its relationship with the local church, and whether it was causing division rather than unity.

This book is born out of those experiences, the good, the bad, and the transformative. Over the years, I've come to see how growth and change, both in individuals and ministries, can bring about tension but also incredible opportunities for collaboration and mutual edification.

What is a Para-church Ministry?

A para-church ministry is an organization that operates alongside local churches, often focusing on specific aspects of Christian service or outreach that may not be fully addressed within the traditional church structure. These ministries complement the work of the local church by filling gaps and meeting specialized needs, such as youth programs, missions, or worship gatherings. Para-church ministries are not meant to replace the church but to serve as partners in advancing the kingdom of God. They exist to extend the reach of the church into areas where its resources or focus may be limited, creating opportunities for collaboration and expanded impact.

Why the Need for a Ministry Within a Ministry?

The dual role of having a ministry within another ministry is both necessary and beneficial. While the local church serves as the primary place for spiritual growth, fellowship, and discipleship, para-church organizations provide an avenue to explore and develop specific callings and gifts that may not fit within the confines of traditional church activities. This relationship between local churches and para-church ministries fosters a dynamic environment where both can thrive.

For example, True Worshippers was born out of a desire to create a space for extended praise and worship, something that time constraints often limited during regular church services. By operating as a para-church ministry, True Worshippers was able to gather believers from various denominations, creating a platform for unity and collaboration. At the same time, the ministry's connection to the local church ensured accountability and alignment with biblical principles.

However, this dynamic is not without challenges. Misunderstandings and insecurities can arise when the purpose of the para-church ministry is not clearly communicated or when its activities are perceived as competition rather than complementing the local church. This book seeks to address these challenges, offering practical guidance on how to navigate the complexities of having a ministry within a ministry while maintaining harmony and unity.

The heart of this book is to explore how one can faithfully steward a ministry within another ministry. How do we navigate the delicate balance of serving another's vision while pursuing the gifts and calling God has placed within us? How can local churches and para-church organizations work in harmony, learning from and growing with each other? These questions aren't just theoretical for me; they're deeply personal. Today, as a pastor in the Church of Pentecost, I stand as a testament to the fact that it is possible to have a thriving para-church ministry without abandoning your local church. But let me be clear—it wasn't easy.

Fifteen years later, True Worshippers has impacted countless lives, but it's also taught me invaluable lessons about humility, partnership, and perseverance. One of the most significant lessons is that having a ministry within a ministry doesn't have to create division or competition. Instead, it can foster unity and growth when approached with the right heart and intentions. This book aims to share those lessons with you.

If you're someone with a gift or calling and find yourself serving another's vision, my prayer is that this book will encourage you to see your role as significant and purposeful. You'll come to understand that it's okay to grow and flourish within the boundaries of another ministry. Not every leader is out to suppress or stifle you. Many pastors and leaders genuinely want to see you succeed, sometimes even beyond what they've achieved. Your challenge is to remain humble, faithful, and willing to learn. But remain sensitive to the leading of the Lord. He may call you out of a ministry, or He may plant you deeper within it, but always let Him lead."

If you're a pastor or church leader, my hope is that this book will give you a fresh perspective on how to shepherd the gifted individuals within your congregation. Instead of seeing their calling as a threat, you'll discover how their unique gifts can complement and enhance the vision God has given you. Insecurity doesn't have to be your default response. By embracing collaboration, you can create an environment where both the local church and para-church ministries thrive together.

As we journey through this book, we'll explore practical principles, biblical truths, and real-life experiences that highlight how ministries can coexist in harmony. We'll also confront the challenges and pitfalls that often arise, offering guidance on how to overcome them with grace and wisdom. Ultimately, my prayer is that this book will equip and inspire you to navigate the complexities of ministry with integrity and faithfulness.

True Worshippers began with a simple vision: to fill a gap in the local church and bring people together to worship God. Over the years, it has grown into something far greater than I could have imagined. Yet, its journey has been anything but smooth. The lessons I've learned along the way have shaped me not just as a leader but as a follower of Christ.

Whether you're a young leader with a burning vision, a seasoned pastor shepherding a congregation, or someone caught between two worlds, this book is for you. Together, let's discover how to honor God's calling on our lives while building His kingdom in unity and love.

01.

The Role of Para-church Ministries

When God placed the vision of True Worshippers Inc. on my heart in 2009, I had little understanding of the broader framework into which this ministry fit. Over the years, I've come to realize that True Worshippers is part of a category of organizations known as para-church ministries. These ministries operate alongside the local church, addressing specific needs or gaps that local congregations may not have the capacity to fulfill fully. But what exactly is a parachurch ministry, and how does it complement the mission of the church?

The term "para-church" comes from the Greek prefix para- meaning "beside" or "alongside." A para-church ministry, therefore, is an organization designed to support and work alongside the local church, extending its reach and meeting specialized needs that the church may not be equipped to address within its normal structure.

These ministries vary in scope and focus. Some address humanitarian needs, such as The Salvation Army, which provides food, shelter, and disaster relief to those in crisis; Samaritan's Purse, which offers emergency relief and aid to impoverished communities around the world; and Mercy Ships, a medical charity that delivers life-changing surgeries aboard floating hospitals. Others, like the YMCA, started as faith-based organizations to serve youth and foster Christian values. Still, others focus on spreading the gospel through creative means like media, publishing, or internet evangelism.

While the local church serves as the foundation of the Christian faith, tasked with building up the body of believers and equipping them for ministry (Ephesians 4:11-12), para-church ministries play a supporting role. They allow believers to focus on specific callings, such as missions, education, or outreach, that may fall outside the church's primary focus.

The Biblical Basis for Supporting Ministries

In Ephesians 4:11-12 (NKJV), Paul writes,

"And He Himself gave some to be apostles, some prophets, some evangelists, and some pastors and teachers, for the equipping of the saints for the work of ministry, for the edifying of the body of Christ".

This passage highlights that the role of church leadership is to equip the saints, believers like you and me, to carry out the work of ministry.

The word "ministry" here is translated from the Greek word diakonia, which originally referred to service, such as waiting tables or performing tasks on behalf of others. This is exemplified in Acts 6:1-5 (NKJV), where the apostles appointed deacons to manage the daily distribution of food so they could focus on prayer and the ministry of the Word:

*"**1** Now in those days, when the number of the disciples was multiplying, there arose a complaint against the Hebrews by the Hellenists, because their widows were neglected in the daily distribution. **2** Then the twelve summoned the multitude of the disciples and said, 'It is not desirable that we should leave the word of God and serve tables. **3** Therefore, brethren, seek out from among you seven men of good reputation, full of the Holy Spirit and wisdom, whom we may appoint over this business; **4** but we will give ourselves continually to prayer and to the ministry of the word.' **5** And the saying pleased the whole multitude..."*

This example illustrates that even in the early church, there was a recognition that certain tasks required delegation to ensure the broader mission of the church could continue effectively. Similarly, para-church ministries often step in to serve where the church cannot due to limited resources, time, or focus.

The Strengths of Para-church Ministries

Para-church ministries offer several benefits that enhance the work of the local church:

Specialization: These organizations focus on specific areas of need, whether it's global missions, youth outreach, or humanitarian aid. For example, Mercy Ships provides surgical care in underserved regions, something most local churches couldn't sustain on their own.

Collaboration: By bringing together believers from diverse denominations, para-church ministries foster unity and cooperation within the broader body of Christ.

Expanded Reach: Through media, publishing, and technology, para-church ministries can spread the gospel to places the local church might not reach, such as closed countries or remote areas. Supplementing Local Church Efforts: They provide additional resources, training, and opportunities for believers to serve, complementing the discipleship and community provided by the church.

The Challenges of Para-church Ministries

While para-church ministries offer immense value, they are not without challenges. One major concern is that these organizations often operate independently of church oversight. Without the accountability of the local church, para-church ministries can drift from sound doctrine or become overly focused on their specific mission to the detriment of the broader gospel message.

Paul reminds Timothy of the church's foundational role in 1 Timothy 3:15:

"...but if I am delayed, I write so that you may know how you ought to conduct yourself in the house of God, which is the church of the living God, the pillar and ground of the truth" (NKJV).

This verse underscores that the local church is the God-ordained institution for teaching, discipling, and upholding the truth. When para-church ministries operate without the guidance of church leadership, they risk losing sight of this foundation.

Another challenge is the potential for doctrinal dilution. Because para-church organizations often draw workers and leaders from various denominations, they may focus on the lowest common denominator of agreement, avoiding controversial but essential doctrines to maintain unity. For example, when a para-church organization gathers volunteers from Baptist, Pentecostal, and Presbyterian backgrounds, they may avoid teaching on topics like speaking in tongues or predestination to prevent conflict. As a result, core biblical teachings are watered down to maintain a surface-level unity. This can lead to a faith expression that is broad but shallow, lacking the depth of essential doctrine.

The Importance of Accountability

To mitigate these challenges, I firmly believe that every para-church ministry should remain under the oversight of a pastor, church, or denomination. God established the church as the spiritual home for believers, providing godly leadership to shepherd the flock, protect against false teaching, and ensure alignment with biblical principles.

When para-church ministries submit to the oversight of a local church, they benefit from spiritual covering, accountability, and a connection to the broader mission of the church. This partnership fosters mutual growth and ensures that the ministry remains aligned with God's purpose.

The bigger issue with many para-church organizations is that they often begin from a place of noticing a lack in the local church. While recognizing these gaps is important, the frustration that comes with it can sometimes lead individuals to start their ministries from a place of reaction rather than contribution. I can relate to this personally. Many young people notice something another church or ministry is doing that their own church is not, and they feel compelled to rise up with a new mission. However, they often do so without consulting their mentors, leaders, or head pastors. They gather people to their cause with the mindset, *This is what my generation needs" or "This is what the church isn't doing, so God is using me to show them."* While these frustrations are real and at times valid, if they are not channeled through the wisdom of the Holy Spirit and senior leaders, the result can be a ministry born out of rebellion rather than grace. *I call it the "I Went, Not Sent" Syndrome, when ministers step out on their own without the affirmation, covering, or commissioning of their local church leadership.* There's a critical difference between being called and being sent. Yes, the call of God may rest on your life from the womb, but the sending requires timing, maturity, and alignment with spiritual authority. David was anointed as king while still a boy, but he wasn't enthroned until fifteen years later. The oil may mark you early, but it's the process and proper release that prepares you to reign well. It's crucial to remember that para-church ministries are meant to come alongside the church, not work against it. This is why they are called para-church ministries:they are designed to partner with the body of Christ to emphasize specific areas the church may not have the resources or time to focus on fully.

I remember a friend asking me why I started True Worshippers. My initial answer started well but ended poorly. I explained that when I led worship at my local church, I often felt frustrated when elders would tap me on the back and tell me my time was up. This constant interruption left me feeling stifled, and I convinced myself that True Worshippers would be a space where worship had no time limits. However, my motivation wasn't entirely pure. It wasn't because I wanted to reflect the heavenly worship of angels singing, *Holy, Holy, Holy is the Lord God Almighty" 24/7.* Instead, I wanted to prove a point to my church leadership. My mindset was, "You don't understand the importance of worship because you limit it, but I'll show you how it should be done."

That frustration-driven mindset wasn't healthy, and it could have easily led to division. Ministries born out of frustration often create tension and, in some cases, lead people to leave their churches altogether. But a para-church ministry must operate with the humility to work alongside the church, not in opposition to it.

A Call to Serve Together

As I reflect on the journey of True Worshippers Inc., I have come to recognize the profound importance of maintaining a strong and visible connection with my local church. This relationship has not only anchored me spiritually but has also established a clear sense of accountability and trust within the broader faith community. One of the most significant benefits of this connection has been the confidence it has inspired in other pastors within the region.

Because I have consistently identified with the Church of Pentecost, a denomination known for its steadfast commitment to biblical doctrine and disciplined leadership, other ministers have felt secure entrusting their members and youth to my ministry. They saw me as a man under authority, someone who operated within a recognized spiritual covering. This assurance meant they were not apprehensive that I might lead their members astray or teach doctrines that would cause confusion. Rather, they knew I was committed to upholding the principles and values of our shared faith tradition.

The Church of Pentecost's reputation for discipline and doctrinal integrity did more than protect relationships; it created a safe environment for collaboration. It allowed me to serve and disciple without suspicion, fostering a culture of mutual respect and cooperation among pastors and leaders.

In a world where independence is often celebrated, I have learned that spiritual alignment with a local church is not a limitation but a platform. It provides a foundation of credibility, a context of accountability, and a community of spiritual covering. And for this reason, I can confidently say that maintaining a close relationship with my local church has been one of the most impactful decisions in my ministry journey.

For those leading or considering starting a para-church ministry, my encouragement is this: Stay connected to your local church. Seek the wisdom and guidance of your pastors and leaders. Allow their input to shape your ministry and keep you grounded in God's Word.

For pastors and church leaders, I urge you to see para-church ministries as partners rather than competitors. When you embrace these organizations and support their vision, you create opportunities for collaboration that can advance the kingdom of God in powerful ways.

As we move forward in this book, we'll explore practical steps for navigating the challenges and opportunities of operating a ministry within a ministry. Whether you're a para-church leader, a pastor, or someone with a dream to serve God in a unique way, I pray this book will equip and inspire you to build God's kingdom in unity and love.

02.

Starting Right

Building Ministry Under Covering

In the previous chapter, we explored what a para-church ministry is, a God-ordained effort that functions alongside the local church to serve specific needs within the Body of Christ. But in this chapter, I want to walk with you through how to start a para-church ministry, whether it's a worship movement, preaching ministry, outreach effort, or even a faith-based organization, while still being faithfully committed to your local church.

Let me say this from the beginning: every true move of God must begin with accountability. Don't bypass the house that fed you to build a tent outside its walls. Start your ministry within your church, not outside of it. Your local church should not be your competitor; it should be your incubator.

Now, you may be someone reading this who has been carrying a vision in your heart for years, unsure how to start. Or maybe you've already launched something, but you're finding it difficult to navigate the "church politics" or gain support. This chapter is for you. My prayer is that it becomes a step-by-step guide and also a mirror to reflect where alignment may be needed.

1. Ministry Begins With Jesus—Not Your Gift

Ministry is not about platforms or popularity; it is always about Jesus and His people. Before anything else, sit with God. Don't just identify your gift—discern your assignment. Every spiritual initiative must be birthed from intimacy with God.

If God has placed something on your heart, ask Him:

- → What is this for?
- → Who is this for?
- → How would You have me begin?

Your clarity must first come from the secret place. However, don't stop there, because God often confirms His will through the spiritual leaders He has placed in your life.

2. Present the Vision With Honor and Preparation

Once God has given you direction, go and see your pastor or church leadership. Don't go empty-handed, come with vision written down. Habakkuk 2:2 tells us to "write the vision and make it plain." Honor is demonstrated not just through words, but through preparedness.

Let your pastor see that you didn't just wake up with an idea, you've prayed, planned, and submitted the matter before the Lord. Present it as someone who is asking for advice, not control. Share the vision, but more importantly, share your willingness to receive counsel and correction.

Let me remind you of 1 Samuel 3:7–11. God was calling the boy Samuel, but it took the wisdom of Eli to help him discern how to respond. Samuel heard the voice of the Lord, yes, but without Eli's instruction, he may have remained confused in the dark.

We need fathers and mothers in the Lord to help us posture ourselves correctly to receive the fullness of God's voice. Sometimes we hear a part, but it is the counsel of leaders that helps us walk in the whole.

3. The Blessing of the Greater

We live in a generation that underestimates the power of a leader's blessing. Don't make that mistake.

Hebrews 7:7 says,

"And without question, the lesser is blessed by the greater."

The author is showing that Melchizedek, a mysterious priest-king who blessed Abraham (Genesis 14), is greater than Abraham himself. Why?

Because:

→ Abraham gave Melchizedek a tithe, and
→ Melchizedek blessed Abraham.

In biblical tradition, only someone greater blesses someone lesser. That's what verse 7 is stating: "The inferior is blessed by the superior." Abraham, though the father of the faith, received a blessing from someone higher in spiritual rank.

The biblical pattern is clear: blessings flow from the top down. Jacob and Esau wrestled for their father's blessing because they understood a principle we often forget, no matter how gifted you are, there are things you will never walk in until someone greater blesses you.

When I started "True Worshippers," I didn't just gather people, I ran to my pastor, Rev. Joseph Akoto, and shared what I believed God had put on my heart. He laid his hands on me and prayed. Even though he wasn't a musical person, he later called me and said, "Yaw, add fasting and prayer. Music alone is not enough, this is spiritual."

That call shifted something. I had been so focused on planning and logistics that I was about to leave out the one thing that would give the event its true power: God's presence. That wisdom came because I submitted the vision. His covering released insight.

4. Accountability Attracts Support

When you build under covering, resources are more likely to follow. My national church gave $1,000 to support the launch of True Worshippers, not because I demanded it, but because leadership was aware, informed, and spiritually aligned with the mission.

Most of my volunteers came from my local church. Why? Because leadership endorsed it. They announced it. They stood behind it. When other pastors in the community heard about it, they not only gave financially, they released people to help. But that only happened because I wasn't viewed as a lone ranger.

Covering brings credibility. Unchecked independence often raises red flags. A ministry with no visible accountability may be perceived as spiritually unsafe even if the vision is powerful.

5. Establish a Structure of Accountability

If you're starting something, consider forming a board of directors or trusted advisors, pastors, mature leaders, or seasoned professionals with character, spiritual insight, and a heart for your assignment. Their role is to speak truth in love, ask hard questions, and help steer your ministry with wisdom.

Even the Godhead operates in accountability. In John 16:13, Jesus says the Holy Spirit "will not speak on His own; He will speak only what He hears." And in 1 Corinthians 11:3, Paul outlines divine order: "The head of Christ is God."

If the Holy Spirit is accountable to the Son, and the Son to the Father, then what makes us think we can move without oversight? Let me ask you plainly: Who are you accountable to, gifted one?

6. Wisdom Makes Ministry Sustainable

Moses was one of the most anointed men in scripture, but it was his father-in-law Jethro, not a prophet, who gave him the leadership strategy that transformed his ministry. (See Exodus 18.)

Jethro observed Moses taking on too much and said, "What you're doing is not good... you will wear yourself out." He gave Moses a system of delegation and structure that preserved him and empowered others.

Jethro's voice reminds us that sometimes the help we need doesn't come from a popular platform but from seasoned eyes watching in love. Submit to that kind of voice. It may not shout, but it will preserve you.

7. Build With Submission, Not Ambition

As you begin or continue building your ministry, remember this: starting something great without accountability is like constructing a house without a foundation. It may stand for a while, but it won't last the storms.

If you want to build something that lasts, submit it. Get the blessing of those above you. Seek wisdom. Invite correction. Create systems of accountability. Surround yourself with people who love God and aren't impressed by your gift.

Your longevity in ministry will not be sustained by talent alone, but by counsel, character, and covering.

You may be anointed like Moses, but if you don't have a Jethro, you will burn out.

You may be called like Samuel, but without an Eli, you may never discern what God is fully saying.

You may be as visionary as Jacob, but without Isaac's blessing, you'll never walk in the fullness of your inheritance.

Reflection Questions

1. Have you submitted your vision to spiritual leadership?

2. Who are your spiritual advisors, and are they free to correct you?

3. Is your ministry covered by intercession and fasting—or just talent?

4. Are you open to feedback from those who have gone before you?

Start well. Build wisely. Stay submitted. And watch God breathe on your obedience.

03.

Eyes to See, Hands to Lift

Every pastor should be watchful for those in their congregation who carry a fire that hasn't yet spread. These are individuals marked by God, carrying untapped potential, waiting to be stewarded and not stifled. Oftentimes, it's those individuals who carry a distinct fire and passion that are the ones who launch para-church organizations or ministries.

Often, tensions arise between pastors and members with emerging ministries because, if we're honest, some pastors operate with a *"me-focused"* lens instead of a *"you-focused"* one. Let me explain.

When a pastor is starting or building a church, the primary focus is often on forming teams and ministries that meet the immediate needs of the church. While that's necessary, it's incomplete. The danger is that we bring people close only to fill roles that serve our vision, without discipling them to discover *God's* vision for their lives.

If we had the foresight to disciple people not just for church function, but for personal formation and Kingdom assignment, we wouldn't be threatened when grace starts to reveal itself in familiar faces. We would celebrate it, steward it, and help them grow into it.

Sometimes it amazes me to consider that Saul had encountered David well before David ever fought and defeated Goliath, Saul's enemy. In 1 Samuel 16:21–23, we clearly see that David was already in Saul's service, playing the harp to soothe Saul when he was tormented by an evil spirit. The Scripture plainly states,

"David came to Saul and entered his service. Saul liked him very much, and David became one of his armor-bearers."

Thus, Saul definitely knew David prior to the battle with Goliath.

Yet, despite David's proximity and service, Saul seemed to use David primarily for his own immediate needs, particularly his personal relief and comfort within the kingdom. David's outstanding character and abilities were clearly highlighted in 1 Samuel 16:18, where one of Saul's servants describes him vividly:

"Look, I have seen a son of Jesse the Bethlehemite, who is skillful in playing, a mighty man of valor, a man of war, prudent in speech, and a handsome person; and the Lord is with him."

With such glowing accolades, Saul had ample evidence of David's remarkable character and abilities.

However, when David defeats Goliath, Saul acts as though he has never truly noticed David before. In 1 Samuel 17:55–58, Saul inquires of Abner, his commander, *"Whose son is this youth?"* and later directly asks David himself, *"Whose son are you, young man?"* This apparent confusion can seem puzzling because Saul had previously summoned David himself, sending messengers directly to Jesse's house.

This scenario reveals a deeper issue: Saul's attention was largely self-focused. He utilized David solely for personal and kingdom benefit, never truly considering David's growth, potential, or broader destiny. Saul's failure to recognize David fully beyond immediate personal advantage eventually led to deep tensions and rivalry.

Ultimately, Saul and David, two men who could have powerfully collaborated for the kingdom's advancement, became adversaries. This outcome serves as a poignant reminder of the dangers pastors face when they lack the discernment and humility to recognize and nurture the greatness and potential within their congregations beyond their personal agendas and immediate ministry needs.

Now, as pastors, our eyes must be open and attentive to those in our congregations who display evident gifts and talents, especially those actively expressing themselves in ministry areas like singing, prayer, preaching, or passionately pursuing spiritual growth. When you see individuals quickly exercising and developing their spiritual gifts, don't hesitate to step in and mentor them personally. Don't allow external voices to exclusively mentor the potential you first recognized. Capturing these individuals early, grants pastors significant liberty and influence in shaping their spiritual and ministerial development.

Proverbs 29:21 underscores a powerful principle in mentorship and leadership:

"He who carefully nurtures his servant from youth will find him becoming like a son in the end."

This proverb teaches that intentional and consistent investment in a gifted individual at an early stage creates deep bonds of loyalty, respect, and enduring influence. When you recognize potential early and nurture it gently and intentionally, the relationship transcends mere transactional service and transforms into a lasting, familial-like bond. This bond solidifies trust and ensures that the mentee remains willingly connected, open to guidance, correction, and continued development under your mentorship.

Capturing gifted individuals early does more than leverage their talents; it cultivates relationships that produce mutual respect, deep loyalty, and a lasting legacy.

Reflecting on my own journey, I began singing as early as second grade. At my former church, Gateway International Christian Church, a minister named Moses Ashun, now Bishop Ashun, recognized my musical gift early and intentionally mentored me. Weekends spent at his home, watching iconic recordings like Donnie McClurkin's "Live in London" album, Clint Brown, Gary Oliver, and Ron Kenoly, became foundational to my development. Minister Moses poured into me not because he sought personal gain but because he genuinely recognized greatness and invested in nurturing it.

When Pastor Moses eventually started his own ministry in Atlanta, I gladly supported him by leading praise and worship, compelled by gratitude and the deep investment he had made in me. Although my schedule was busy, remembering his mentorship inspired me to prioritize his ministry. This experience illustrates powerfully how pastors who invest in their members create individuals who readily and joyfully offer their gifts to advance the kingdom agenda. Such members welcome pastoral guidance, mentorship, and wisdom for their personal ministries, strengthening the entire body of Christ.

As pastors, we must understand that we cannot expect to direct what we haven't first influenced. The era of relying solely on positional authority, authority based purely on titles and hierarchical power, is fading. Today's generation responds more powerfully to relational authority, built on genuine influence, trust, and authentic relationships.

One thing that has often puzzled me about our approach as men and women of God toward gifted individuals in our churches is our tendency to observe them skeptically from a distance. We frequently remain silent until we feel compelled to speak up when something appears wrong or problematic. Instead, why not proactively encourage these gifted individuals, highlighting their strengths and offering constructive feedback that can guide and improve their ministry?

I recall a friend who had an interdenominational prayer ministry yet remained a faithful member of the Assemblies of God. Every few months, he hosted packed prayer gatherings. Despite inviting his pastor and fellow church members regularly, his pastor would consistently decline the invitations and subtly influence members to do the same. The pastor disapproved of my friend's style and felt the prayer topics lacked solid biblical grounding and was "too Charismatic".

Eventually, a guest prophet invited to speak at one of these events delivered prophecies that were considered overly explicit. News quickly reached the pastor, prompting a confrontational meeting where the pastor harshly criticized my friend, accusing him of rushing into ministry and insisting that any ministry efforts should be submitted fully to the church.

My friend's response was profound and unforgettable:

> *"Why would I submit my ministry to someone who clearly doesn't support me? You only engage with me when things go wrong. You've never positively contributed or provided guidance when I've invited you, so why should I entrust my ministry to someone who doesn't even like me?"*

This sobering moment led the pastor to realize his mistake. He saw the young man's potential clearly and understood his role in neglecting a gifted individual who could benefit both personally and corporately from genuine pastoral guidance.

Realizing this, the pastor apologized and began intentionally nurturing a healthy, collaborative relationship with my friend. Today, the result of that shift is remarkable: attendees of the prayer ministry have started attending the Assemblies of God church on Sundays, recognizing authentic mentorship, correction, and collaboration. The pastor now regularly preaches at these gatherings, attracting new congregants drawn by the fruitful relationship they witness.

This story underscores a critical lesson: We must proactively identify and nurture gifted individuals, building authentic relationships and mentoring them faithfully. When we do, their growth becomes our blessing, and our mentorship becomes their foundation, fostering mutual benefit and kingdom advancement.

We see this done with Aquila, Priscilla, and Apollos (Acts 18:24-28). Apollos was gifted yet needed further grounding. Aquila and Priscilla privately mentored him, demonstrating proactive and constructive mentorship without public embarrassment or harsh criticism.

"...They took him aside and explained to him the way of God more accurately." —Acts 18:26 (ESV)

Because of their intentional mentorship and encouragement, Apollos became a profoundly effective minister, recognized by Paul himself for his eloquence and impact (1 Corinthians 3:5-6). Their relational investment transformed Apollo's potential into powerful kingdom influence.

Ultimately, wise pastoral leadership sees potential as a divine trust, stewarding it carefully rather than stifling or exploiting it. True shepherds proactively nurture emerging leaders not merely for immediate church needs, but for kingdom impact and personal fulfillment in Christ. When pastors cultivate authentic, relational authority, their churches become spiritual families where greatness is celebrated rather than feared. May we be leaders who gladly raise up sons and daughters in ministry, discipling them faithfully so that their fire spreads far beyond our own vision, for the glory of God and the good of His Kingdom.

04.

Anointed, But Yet Accountable

L et me begin this chapter with a bold statement, which may initially seem polarizing, but allow me a moment to explain myself clearly: For gifted individuals serving in the church, your greatest battles will likely not arise from external forces in the world but from within the church itself. Yes, I said it, your most significant challenges and tensions will often stem from within the very place intended for your growth and spiritual nourishment.

Some of these internal battles you face may come without any provocation on your part, simply a result of envy, misunderstanding, or insecurity among others. Yet, if we are completely honest, other conflicts emerge because of your own immaturity, lack of wisdom, or unchecked ambition. To explore this point thoroughly, let us closely examine the life of David, whose most defining struggles emerged not on the battlefield, but within the very palace he called home.

David indeed encountered dangerous adversaries outside, lions, bears, and the giant Goliath. Yet, these external threats were clear and identifiable, allowing David to prepare and respond accordingly. But David's greatest challenges arose from places of intimacy, familiarity, and trust: Saul, Bathsheba, and Absalom. Each of these crises occurred within the palace, highlighting how proximity and relationship intensify pain and   complexity.

Consider Saul, who threw spears at David in the palace, intending to kill him. Scripture recounts this vividly:

"The next day a harmful spirit from God rushed upon Saul, and he raved within his house while David was playing the lyre, as he did day by day. Saul had his spear in his hand. And Saul hurled the spear, for he thought, 'I will pin David to the wall." —1 Samuel 18:10–11 (ESV)

But David evaded him twice:

"Then a harmful spirit from the Lord came upon Saul, as he sat in his house with his spear in his hand. And David was playing the lyre. And Saul sought to pin David to the wall with the spear, but he eluded Saul, so that he struck the spear into the wall. And David fled and escaped that night." —1 Samuel 19:9–10 (ESV)

The temptation and subsequent fall involving Bathsheba likewise unfolded within the palace walls:

"It happened, late one afternoon, when David arose from his couch and was walking on the roof of the king's house, that he saw from the roof a woman bathing; and the woman was very beautiful." — 2 Samuel 11:2 (ESV)

The account of Absalom openly dishonoring his father by sleeping with David's concubines on the palace rooftop is vividly captured in 2 Samuel 16:22 (ESV):

"So they pitched a tent for Absalom on the roof, and Absalom went into his father's concubines in the sight of all Israel."

This deeply troubling incident illustrates how even those closest to us, people we trust and positions we cherish, can become the source of our greatest pain and most complex challenges. The palace, typically a symbol of security and honor, unexpectedly became a place of humiliation, betrayal, and public disgrace for David.

Yet, the story of David profoundly reminds us that God is sovereign even amid chaos. The unexpected conflicts and trials arising within the walls we thought safe are often God's tools for molding our character, deepening our accountability, and refining our ministries. Though painful, these moments teach us humility and reliance on God, transforming our hearts to prioritize His desires above our own ambitions and comforts, even when His ways seem incomprehensible to us.

Let us consider the story of David a bit more deeply. Notice carefully that even though King Saul threw a spear at David, David merely evaded the spear without retaliating. This is an essential lesson I want to highlight for young leaders and people with ministries: do not retaliate in kind when mistreated, especially by those placed in authority over you. Remember, whoever is above you is positioned there by God Himself. Saul, despite his fleshly and hostile behavior, was still God's anointed king. David recognized this and refrained from returning harm for harm.

Moreover, it is crucial to realize that not all leadership lessons come from what your pastor or leader explicitly tells you. Many valuable lessons come from observing their actions, both good and bad. Indeed, one of the greatest leadership insights is identifying what you see your leaders doing that you would resolve never to emulate. Had David killed Saul when he had the chance, considering David's renowned skill and courage (this is the same David who defeated Goliath with a single stone), David would never have learned the crucial lesson of avoiding Saul's mistakes as king. Sometimes, God positions us near spiritual "fathers and mothers" not just to learn from their strengths but equally from their weaknesses. Observing their flaws helps us commit deeply within ourselves never to repeat those errors.

There was a season in my life when I had just released some new singles, and as a result, I was being invited to minister and sing at various churches. This often meant I missed Sunday services at my local church. My pastor would frequently ask my presiding elder, "Where is

Yaw?" and the elder would inform him that I was away ministering. Eventually, I heard that my pastor was quite upset about my frequent absences and had expressed his frustration to others, feeling that my ministry trips weren't producing any real fruit. While I now understand his perspective more clearly, at the time, I was hurt— especially because he never addressed the issue with me directly.

Fast forward to today, I now pastor many young people. One young choir member, incredibly talented and anointed, frequently traveled to minister alongside renowned gospel artists without informing me. I found myself in the pastor's position, repeatedly asking my leaders, "Where is our singer?" At that moment, I vividly recalled how my former pastor's indirect approach had wounded me. Determined not to replicate that error, I proactively reached out to her.

In our conversation, I gently instructed her on proper ministry etiquette while serving under pastoral leadership. I advised her to maintain clear communication and an organized schedule, sharing it with her pastor to ensure accountability and pastoral covering. Recognizing the importance of the local church, I encouraged her to prioritize attending services regularly, ideally at least two Sundays a month. I also emphasized the necessity of knowing significant church events and making every effort to support them, especially during busy ministry seasons. We also discussed how I could support her music ministry by connecting her with influential and trusted individuals who could help her grow and thrive in her calling.

Our honest dialogue significantly strengthened our relationship and enhanced the effectiveness of our local church's ministry, as well as her personal ministry endeavors. This encounter taught me profoundly: rather than retaliating or distancing ourselves when hurt or misunderstood by leadership, we must choose humility and communication.

So, to every young minister or emerging leader: resist the urge to throw spears back at leaders who wound or frustrate you. Stay rooted, learn diligently, and allow God to shape your character through difficult circumstances. Instead of attacking or withdrawing from leadership when offended, focus on killing your own tendencies to repeat their mistakes. By doing this, you transform personal pain into profound wisdom and lasting strength.

How to Make Your Gift or Ministry Accountable to Your Local Church Leadership

1. Communication: Clarity Prevents Conflict

Never leave your pastor guessing. Assumption is a silent killer of relationships, and Scripture shows us that even God Himself does not deal in assumption.

"Then the Lord said, 'Because the outcry against Sodom and Gomorrah is great and their sin is very grave, I will go down to see whether they have done altogether according to the outcry that has come to me. And if not, I will know.'" — Genesis 18:20–21 (ESV)

If the omniscient God chose to "come down" to verify, how much more should we ensure we communicate clearly? If you have a calendar of ministry events, travel dates, or speaking engagements, don't keep it to yourself. Sit down with your pastor, present your plans, and welcome feedback. This not only prevents schedule clashes but also shows honor and accountability.

Another sensitive area is finances. If your ministry is fundraising, especially among members of your local church, communicate clearly with your pastor. Miscommunication about donors or financial campaigns can create confusion and damage trust. If both you and your church are drawing from the same financial well, there must be agreement, not competition. Let communication be so strong that unity is preserved even in sensitive matters.

2. Involvement: Share the Grace That Covers You

A powerful way to honor your pastor is to intentionally involve them in your ministry when appropriate. Invite them to speak, bless your participants, or simply attend. If you draw wisdom, covering, and grace from your pastor's well, it's only right that others connected to you also drink from that same source.

This involvement does more than just show honor, it invites their heart into your work. When a pastor sees that they're not just a figurehead but a valued voice, they become more invested in your growth and your fruitfulness. Their presence affirms your alignment and builds trust in both directions.

3. Wisdom: Build with Counsel, Not Just Charisma

The Bible is clear:

"Plans fail for lack of counsel, but with many advisers they succeed." —Proverbs 15:22 (NIV)

Every para-church ministry or personal calling should have a board or circle of advisors, people who bring spiritual maturity, practical experience, and sound judgment. And yes, your pastor should be one of them. Not to control your vision, but to help refine it.

There's an old African proverb that says, *"What an elder sees sitting down, a child cannot see even if he climbs a tree."* In other words, wisdom is not just about sight, it's about perspective. Your pastor's years of ministry, scars from past battles, and lessons from their journey can help you avoid unnecessary pain and accelerate your growth. Having them in your corner isn't just respectful, it's strategic.

4. Submission: Accountability Requires Mutual Trust

Submission is not slavery, it's safety. When you willingly submit your gift to spiritual authority, you are not losing your voice; you are gaining covering. Your pastor's role is not to stifle your anointing but to shepherd it, protect it, and at times challenge it for your own good.

True accountability doesn't wait until there's a problem to check in. It builds consistent, transparent rhythms of communication, honor, and partnership. The result? A ministry that doesn't just bless people, but one that has longevity, fruitfulness, and the commendation of both man and God.

Don't make the mistake of asking for your pastor's support publicly while avoiding their input privately. Let your ministry be built in the light of accountability, not the shadows of independence. When the house is aligned, the oil flows without obstruction.

05.

Accountability Protects the Anointed

Whenever you are entrusted with a successful para-church organization, ministry, or gift that draws attention, influence, and spiritual impact, remember this sobering truth: your greatest enemy is not the devil. In fact, it is your flesh. The second greatest enemy is indeed Satan, but he only exploits what your flesh has already compromised.

In 1 Peter 5:8, the apostle gives a warning tailor-made for leaders and ministers:

*"Be **sober-minded**; be watchful. Your adversary the devil prowls around like a roaring lion, seeking **someone** to devour."*

There are two key phrases in this passage that every anointed servant of God must take seriously: *"sober-minded"* and *"someone."*

To be sober-minded means to be moderate, disciplined, emotionally balanced, and spiritually alert. It is the opposite of being intoxicated by fame, flattery, ambition, or entitlement. In other words, to be sober-minded is to resist the seduction of elevation. It means refusing to let the applause of men dull your discernment or inflate your ego.

Young ministers, especially those who are gifted and rising quickly, must cling to this posture. Why? Because success, if not governed by sobriety, becomes a gateway to pride. And pride is not only the oldest sin, it is the quickest way for the devil to gain access to your ministry. That's why we must never boast in humility when we've never had the kind of exposure, finances, or platform that test it.

The second word is "someone." Peter didn't say the devil devours everyone, he devours someone. That someone is usually the individual who has allowed their flesh to go unchecked. The one who is gifted but unaccountable. The one who has talent but no anchor. The one who is anointed but isolated.

The truth is: Satan tailors temptations.

Isaiah 54:17 says: *"fashioned against you shall succeed..."*

Pay attention: "fashioned" means formed, shaped, or crafted with intention. That means the weapon formed against you is custom-designed, not generic. It fits your unique vulnerabilities, past wounds, and personality traits. The enemy doesn't waste ammunition; he studies patterns and designs attacks that suit your weaknesses.

This is why accountability isn't optional for the anointed, it's essential. A good pastor, mentor, or spiritual leader isn't just someone who celebrates your gift; they are someone who watches overyour soul *(Hebrews 13:17)*. They help detect spiritual blind spots, confront your flesh, and remind you that ministry is not performance, it's stewardship.

To pastors and leaders: when you oversee gifted individuals who begin traveling, singing, preaching, or organizing events, do not simply cheer them on from a distance. Schedule consistent spiritual and emotional check-ins. The road is filled with hidden traps, admirers, lavish accommodations, large honorariums, and subtle suggestions that turn ministry into an industry.

You must pastor the whole person, not just the public gift.

I'll never forget the wisdom of Pastor Sam Nana Yeboah. When I was a younger minister, he would invite me to preach in Buffalo, New York, but he also watched me closely. Not in suspicion, but in spiritual love. If I lingered too long in conversation with a woman after service, he would call me over under the pretense of needing something and quietly say:

"A minister should not be found in long, aimless conversation with the opposite sex. The longer you talk without purpose, the more likely you'll drift into the wrong conversation, and eventually the wrong conduct."

That was wisdom not control. And it saved me.

Pastor Sam wasn't just trying to make me a great preacher, he wanted me to be a godly man. Before I got married, he gave me counsel that still shapes my home today. He said:

"Don't just come home—call home. Ask your wife if she needs anything before you arrive. Let her know you are thinking of her. That's not just husbandry; that's humility."

What a lesson. Because a good pastor sharpens the gift. But a great pastor shepherds the whole life.

If you are anointed, don't travel alone. If you are gifted, don't grow without guidance. If you are successful, don't stop being sober minded.

The flesh is subtle, and the enemy is strategic. But with spiritual accountability, pastoral covering, and a heart that stays low before God, you can be gifted and preserved.

Because the goal is not just starting well. It's finishing as faithful.

06.

Voices

The fall of mankind didn't begin with violence or bloodshed. It didn't start with Cain killing Abel. No, it began with a voice.

It was the voice of the serpent, subtle, suggestive, and strategic, that drew Eve's attention, stirred her curiosity, and ultimately led to her disobedience. That one conversation changed the trajectory of humanity. The curse that afflicted the earth and the pain that entered childbirth began with a voice, not a weapon.

This pattern still plays out today. Voices, well-intended or malicious, have the power to shift perception, distort relationships, and plant seeds of division. Voices have been the unseen force behind the breakdown of trust between pastors and their mentees, between leaders and rising gifts within their churches.

We see a vivid example in 1 Samuel 18:7 (ESV):

"And the women sang to one another as they celebrated, 'Saul has struck down his thousands, and David his ten thousands.'"

What should have been a national celebration turned into a personal offense. Saul heard the voices of the people and internalized them, not as honor to David, but as a threat to himself. That single chant became the crack in Saul's soul that allowed jealousy, fear, and suspicion to take root.

And what happened to Saul still happens in many churches today. A young man or woman in the church begins to gain traction. Their ministry is bearing fruit, people are being helped, testimonies are spreading, even outside the four walls of the church. Suddenly, voices arise:

> *"Have you seen Brother So-and-So's prayer call? It's powerful."*

> *"Sis really carries an anointing... sometimes I feel more from her than I do on Sundays."*

> *"People are tuning into her livestreams more than the church service."*

Now the voices reach leadership. Some say, "Pastor, you may want to be careful... the people are starting to follow this one more than the house." What began as a work of grace becomes clouded by suspicion, not because of rebellion, but because of whispered fears.

But let us be sober and discerning. Not every rising gift is a threat. Sometimes, they are the help we've been praying for. God may send someone younger or differently anointed to address areas in our church we've struggled with, healing, deliverance, prophetic ministry, administration, or evangelism. Their presence is not an indictment of our calling, it's an extension of God›s mercy.

For example, a pastor might be called as a teacher, sound in doctrine, rich in word, but perhaps lacking in healing grace. Then God places a faithful member in the house with a healing anointing. That's not competition, that's completion. But if voices cause us to misinterpret help as harm, we end up rejecting what God sent to expand us.

Guard your ears, protect your eyes. Pastors and leaders must be careful with conversations, especially the subtle ones. Not every "concern" shared with you is constructive. Some voices come wrapped in loyalty but are soaked in fear and control. If you›re not discerning, you'll begin to see a blessing as a burden, and a gift as a threat.

Let us not be naïve, the voices don't only come for the pastor, they come for the gifted servant too. Those rising in favor, those whose ministries are bearing visible fruit while still under the covering of a local church, often become targets of subtle whispers and dangerous praise.

When God begins to use you publicly, people will gather, not always to celebrate, but sometimes to manipulate. You'll hear voices saying things like,

"Why don't you go start your own thing?"

"Can't you see how much people adore your ministry?"

"If you left today, half the church would follow you."

These are not compliments, they are seeds of division dressed as encouragement.

And while they whisper to you, another storm is forming behind the scenes. The very pastor who once opened his pulpit to you, affirmed your gift, and created room for your expression, may now be wrestling with internal questions of loyalty. He may begin to sense betrayal, not because of your actions, but because of the perception voices have created around your presence.

But hear this clearly: those who encourage you to walk away in rebellion are not the ones you should walk with into purpose. Why? Because they lack spiritual discernment, and they fail the test of loyalty. Just because someone shares your frustration does not mean they share God's vision for your life.

As a young minister, you must learn to distinguish between sentiment and assignment. We are not led by emotions, we are led by revelation. Even if you are being mishandled or misunderstood by leadership, your posture must remain rooted in honor and divine timing.

Remember David. He didn't promote himself. He didn't gather sympathizers to rebel. He didn't plant a counter-army. He stayed, until staying became a matter of survival.

"And Saul spoke to Jonathan his son and to all his servants, that they should kill David." —1 Samuel 19:1 (ESV)

Only then did David leave, and even in leaving, he wept, because his heart was still with the house he once served.

Sometimes, the very voices that seem to care are driven by a deeper motive—to maintain their own influence with the pastor by sowing doubt about you. These are the voices that want to insulate their position, not protect yours. Don›t be moved by them. Be anchored.

Even Jesus, yes, the sinless Son of God, had to deal with conflicting voices. John the Baptist, His forerunner, the one who once declared,

"Behold, the Lamb of God who takes away the sin of the world" (John 1:29), later sends a question that reveals doubt:

"Are You the one who is to come, or shall we look for another?" —Matthew 11:3 (ESV)

Imagine the weight of that moment. One of the most trusted voices in His life now questions His identity and mission. Yet, Jesus did not spiral. He responded with confidence and clarity:

"Go and tell John what you hear and see: the blind receive their sight, the lame walk, lepers are cleansed, the deaf hear, the dead are raised up, and the poor have good news preached to them." —Matthew 5–11:4 (ESV)

Jesus never let influential voices override divine direction. He wasn't worried about public perception—only about pleasing the One He submitted to: the Father.

As ministers with ministries under covering, our primary concern must be the same. Ask yourself: "Am I aligned with my heavenly Father? Am I submitted and transparent with my spiritual covering?"

If you're walking in both, you don't need to defend yourself from whispers in the dark. Let the fruit speak.

Even when Jesus asked His disciples in Matthew 16, "Who do men say that I am?", the street voices said He was Elijah, John the Baptist, or another prophet. But Peter, by revelation, declared:

"You are the Christ, the Son of the living God."

Jesus responded with confidence:

"Flesh and blood has not revealed this to you, but My Father in heaven."

He knew who He was, not because of external affirmation, but because of divine confirmation.

The Voice That Silences All Others

I'll never forget the year 2019, right in the heart of the pandemic when the whole world was on lockdown and churches were forced to go digital. Everything was live streamed, Facebook Lives, Instagram Lives, Zoom prayer meetings. In the midst of all this, something remarkable happened: True Worshippers began to explode. Our reach grew rapidly. What started as a worship gathering became a global voice of prayer, worship, and encounter, even while the world stood still.

Around the same time, I had just moved back from Texas to Maryland. I had recently gotten married, and as a new husband, thoughts about our future began to stir, where would we raise our family? What kind of church culture would help us grow as a couple and raise godly children? It made sense to explore. We visited pastors who were planting churches, hoping to find a space where our family could thrive spiritually and socially. And as we visited, one thought kept repeating in my mind:

> *"Why not start a True Worshippers church? It's thriving. The momentum is here." And then the voices came.*

Friends, well-meaning and excited, kept saying things like, "Bro, you need to ride this wave. True Worshippers is hot right now. Launch your own thing. It's time to move on from your church and build your own."

To be honest, it made sense in the natural. The growth was evident. The hunger was real. And the temptation was strong. But thank God for a praying wife who said, "Let's not move yet, let's seek God first."

We fasted and prayed for several days. And during that time, I heard nothing. No confirmation. No release. Just silence. Still, we went to church that Sunday, and I quietly thought to myself, "This might be our last service here." But in the middle of worship, boom,

I heard God speak.

Not through a prophet. Not through a friend. Not through a feeling.

I heard His voice.

And it was clear:

>*"Start a PIWC in D.C."*

It wasn't what I expected. It wasn't what others were suggesting. But it was unmistakably God.

And the moment I heard Him, all the other voices went silent. One word from God will silence a thousand opinions.

From that day forward, I moved in obedience—not to ambition, but to assignment. That's how Capital City Church – COP was born. And over the last few years, God has done more than I could have asked or imagined. We remained faithful to the Church of Pentecost's vision, and we continued to host the True Worshippers Conference annually without compromise. One did not cancel the other, they complemented each other.

But let me be honest, the journey wasn't easy.

Even while serving faithfully under COP, some voices within leadership began to question our motives. Rumors started.

> *"They're using the church as a platform to start their own thing."*

The suspicion hurt deeply. We were pouring everything into the church, time, money, prayer, sacrifice, and still, we were misunderstood. It got so painful at times I asked myself, "Why are we killing ourselves for a vision if people don't even trust our heart?" And I'll admit it, I let the hurt get to me. I spoke out of pain. I said things I regret. I vented more than I prayed. But thank God for growth. Thank God for maturity that teaches you not just to bear fruit, but to let your fruit speak when your words fail. Like David, we chose not to throw spears back. We let the work speak.

And now, by the grace of God, the fruit is undeniable. Lives are being changed. Disciples are being formed. The vision is advancing. Not because we followed the voices of men, but because we followed the voice of God.

Do not let any other voice call you out of what God has called you into.

Don't let popularity push you prematurely. Don't let pain pull you off course. And don't let praise from people become the confirmation you move by.

"...My sheep know my voice [21]... and a stranger they will not follow [5]." —John 10:21 and John 10:5

Serve faithfully. Build prayerfully. Submit humbly. And move only when God speaks. Do this work unto the Lord, not for applause, not for opportunity, but for His glory alone.

Because when God calls you, He will carry you, and His voice will always lead you into purpose, not pride.

In a world full of noise, the only voice worth building your life around is the voice of the One who called you. When God speaks, He not only gives direction—He brings peace, clarity, and the strength to endure misunderstanding. Let your obedience outlive their opinions, and let your fruit outlast their suspicions. Stay low, stay faithful, and let heaven—not hype—define your next step. Because in the end, it won't be the voices that validate you—it will be the voice that sent you.

07.

Commitment Issues

When I was younger, one of the most frequent complaints I heard from my local church leaders was that I invested far more time and energy into True Worshippers than into our church's youth programs, especially during Youth Week or choir-related events. At first, I reacted defensively: I assumed they simply didn't understand how much effort it took to pull off something as large as True Worshippers. But in hindsight, I recognize there was truth in their words. I poured relentless passion into fundraising, marketing, and organizing for True Worshippers, yet my church assignments often felt secondary, almost an afterthought.

The root of that disparity was control: with True Worshippers, I felt empowered to shape every detail. I chose the artists, designed the marketing strategy, and determined the program flow. In contrast, church events feltmoreconstrainedbyexistingstructuresanddecision-making hierarchies. I suspect my pastor noticed too that when I promoted my own event, it appeared polished and well-funded, whereas our church's conferences and worship nights felt more "basic." Instead of admitting this, I wallowed in defensiveness, convinced my efforts outside would vindicate me someday.

Then one morning, as I was praying, the Holy Spirit spoke to my heart: "Why not invest that same dedication into your pastor's vision? Where can you serve him sacrificially?" Those words stung, because I'd been reluctant to surrender that "control" I so valued. But as 1 Peter 4:10 reminds us,

"Each of you should use whatever gift you have received to serve others, as faithful stewards of God's grace."

I realized that if I truly wanted to honor my pastor—and mature in humility, I needed to step into his ministry gaps, not simply pursue my own.

So I drove to my pastor's house one afternoon and said, "Pastor, I want to help you plan the next praise-and-worship conference. I know music isn't your strongest area, but I believe our people need this." His eyes lit up. He admitted he'd always wanted someone to carry that burden, but had been unsure where to start. From that moment, I treated his conference with the same zeal I once reserved for True Worshippers: I drafted a marketing plan, coordinated the program schedule, secured worship leaders, and leveraged the relationships I'd built through

True Worshippers to bring quality artists to our church. By God's grace, the event was a resounding success, our first praise conference that was both well-attended and fully funded.

Because I had poured myself into my pastor's vision, everything changed. From then on, whenever I needed support for my own True Worshippers events,whether it was access to the venue or a recommendation to a sponsor, my pastor and church family opened their doors and wallets without hesitation. For example, whereas the church normally charged for building usage, they waived those fees entirely for my personal events, recognizing that I had already "given" sacrificially when it mattered most. In that exchange, I learned that genuine partnership is not about holding power, it's about laying down control, serving faithfully, and trusting God to multiply our efforts for His glory.

Whenever you develop a ministry of your own while also serving in your local church, questions about priorities and commitment will inevitably arise. To prevent these concerns from overshadowing your calling, you must be intentional about balancing your time and energy between both spheres. In practical terms, this means carefully tracking your calendar: if your personal ministry has a particularly demanding season, fundraising drives, conference planning, or outreach campaigns, communicate that well in advance so your church leaders know what to expect. As you navigate those busy stretches, remember Galatians 6:10:

"So then, as we have opportunity, let us do good to everyone, and especially to those who are of the household of faith."

Even when you're stretched thin, look for ways to bless your church family, whether that's arriving early to help set up or sending a brief update to let them know how they can pray for you.

When you are present at church, be fully engaged. Resist the temptation to schedule a major event for your ministry on the same day (or even the same week) as a significant church gathering, doing so sends a message of competition rather than cooperation. A para-church ministry exists to complement and strengthen the local congregation, not to eclipse it. For instance, if your church's annual worship conference is set for the first weekend in October, move your own event to a different weekend or time slot. If your ministry's fundraising banquet falls within Youth Week at church, consider whether you can postpone or delegate some tasks so that you can still lead Bible study on Wednesday night.

Beyond scheduling, cultivate a heart of servanthood toward your pastor and elders. One of the most powerful questions you can ask is, "Pastor, how can I help you?" Far too often, we approach church leaders with our lists of needs, prayers, financial support, promotional assistance, yet seldom do we turn the tables and ask, *"What can I do for you?"* By asking that single question, and then following through, you demonstrate that your loyalty lies first with the local church. Your willingness to fill gaps in worship planning, outreach coordination, or even administrative tasks becomes a tangible expression of love for your church family. Over time, this sacrificial attitude will transform your relationship with church leadership: they'll celebrate your ministry initiatives because they know you have already invested in theirs.

In every season, whether your own ministry demands more attention or your church needs extra hands, keep communication transparent and consistent. Admit when you need to step back, and pledge to return fully engaged as soon as possible. When you serve *"like one who has been shown mercy"* (Romans 12:1), you not only honor God's household but also model the unity Christ intended. In doing so, your ministry will not compete with the church; it will flow alongside it, strengthening both your individual calling and the broader mission of the body of Christ.

When you reach a level of influence or recognition that eclipses, even temporarily, your local church, it can create tension or suspicion if not handled with intentional humility. People may whisper that you're "bigger than the church," or worse, that you've become rebellious. To prevent that, remember these guiding principles:

1. Follow Jesus' Example of Complete Submission

Even as He ministered in Galilee and crowds began to flock to Him, Jesus never allowed public acclaim to derail His mission. In John 5:19 (ESV), He declares:

"Truly, truly, I say to you, the Son can do nothing of His own accord, but only what He sees the Father doing. For whatever the Father does, that the Son does likewise."

Notice two things here:

1. **Dependence on the Father's Voice:** Jesus didn't chart His own course. He sensed the Father's leading in every step, teaching, healing, praying and refused to act apart from that guidance.

2. **Humility in the Midst of Fame:** Although crowds praised Him as a prophet and healer, He never chased human glory. Instead, He withdrew for quiet prayer (Mark 1:35; Luke 5:16), continually realigning with the Father's heart.

If God raises you in prominence, guard your heart with the same posture of submission. Philippians 2:3-4 (ESV) says,

"Do nothing from selfish ambition or conceit, but in humility count others more significant than yourselves. Let each of you look not only to his own interests, but also to the interests of others."

Let that truth fuel your humility: no matter how far God elevates you, keep asking, "What is the Father saying?" and, "How can I serve even now?"

2. Maintain Consistency in Your Local Church Responsibilities

When your personal ministry schedule grows demanding, radio interviews, conference invitations, or international tours, don't let church commitments slip. Your presence in ordinary church life builds trust and demonstrates loyalty. For example:

→ **Choir and Worship Teams:** If you have a thriving music ministry but still sing in your home church's choir, show up consistently and on time for rehearsals. Don't just arrive when you're the featured soloist; come prepared to blend your voice with the congregation every Sunday.

→ **Local Preaching & Prophetic Ministry:** Even if you're invited to preach internationally, make it a point to support fellow ministers back home. Attend baptism services, youth gatherings, or outreach events, even when you aren't on the program. These small sacrifices convey, "My church family matters."

Such acts may feel trivial when you're busy, but they communicate commitment.

By faithfully serving behind the scenes, you reinforce that your identity is rooted in Christ and in your local body, not in public acclaim.

3. Communicate Proactively with Your Pastor and Leadership

When an invitation arrives, whether to host an event or appear on a conference stage, keep your pastor informed. One practical habit I adopted was sending my pastor every official invitation I received, asking, "Pastor, is this okay with you?"

→ **Why This Matters:** You're showing respect for his oversight. If there's an unavoidable conflict, he can speak up, otherwise, his silent blessing becomes a powerful endorsement.

→ **Result:** Pastors feel trusted rather than sidelined. And because you've demonstrated transparency, they'll be eager to open doors for your initiatives.

Proverbs 15:22 (ESV) says, *"Without counsel plans fail, but with many advisers they succeed."*

By inviting your pastor into the conversation, you gain wisdom and avoid hidden resentments. Over time, this collaboration cements unity rather than breeding suspicion.

4. Give Glory First to God, and Then to Your Church

Whenever you minister outside your home church, establish two foundational practices:

1. **Declare God's Supremacy:** Begin by exalting Jesus, His name alone is worthy of our highest praise. This keeps your audience's focus where it belongs.

2. **Acknowledge Your Local Church Family:** Publicly say, "I serve under Pastor Smith at Grace Fellowship, and they have been my spiritual covering." By honoring your senior leadership, you demonstrate that your gifts are not self-generated but poured out from a local body of believers.

When you minister on a larger platform, let your words and actions reflect that you serve Christ through your local church. This posture diffuses jealous whispers and cements your reputation as someone who honours both heaven and the community of faith that raised you.

5. Stay Diligent When "Success" Increases Pressure

As your influence grows, so can the temptation toward pride. You might think, "They need me more than I need this rehearsal," or "My next big event is more important than small-group attendance." Resist these lies.

Pressing on in the "ordinary" choir practice, small groups, Sunday morning set-up, keeps you grounded. These seemingly mundane moments are actually your training ground for greater assignments. Remember: a ministry that bypasses its local church often loses its foundation. People may applaud you from afar, but if you forsake your home base, you risk becoming a floating star, bright yet ungroomed.

In Summary

When your personal ministry begins to outshine your church home:

1. **Submit daily to the Father**—remain dependent, not self-driven (John 5:19; Phil 2:3–4).

2. **Show up faithfully**—sing in the choir, attend rehearsals, and back up your local worship team even when you're in demand elsewhere.

3. **Communicate transparently**—send every invitation to your pastor, seeking his blessing and counsel (Proverbs 15:22).

4. **Give God the ultimate glory** and credit your local church for your growth (Col 3:23–24).

5. **Persevere in the "small" tasks**—they cultivate humility and character for whatever God has next (Heb 12:1–2).

By practicing these disciplines, you deflect criticism, deepen your relationships, and ensure that your expanding influence remains anchored in humble obedience, just as Jesus modeled throughout His earthly ministry.

08.

Leaving Without Wounding

While reading this book, I know a burning question may be rising in your heart: "Pastor Yaw, what do I do when my pastor doesn't like me? I feel like he wants me out of the church." Trust me, I understand the pain, confusion, and deep sense of injustice that can come from serving under leadership that seems hostile or indifferent toward you. I've seen it. I've felt it. But as I've explained throughout these chapters, the answer is not to fight. It's to walk honorably. Even when you feel unseen, mishandled, or misjudged, do everything with integrity and reverence.

You must understand that emotions are unreliable companions in the midst of church conflict. Pain has a way of distorting our discernment, and offense can cloud our spiritual judgment. This is why you must never allow your feelings to become your guide when dealing with difficulty in leadership. Yes, things can get incredibly painful. But remember the example of David and Saul.

Saul's treatment of David was cruel, unjust, and violent. Yet David never retaliated. Why? Because David understood something many of us forget: "Touch not the Lord's anointed."

In 1 Samuel 24:6 (ESV), David told his men, *"The Lord forbid that I should do this thing to my lord, the Lord's anointed, to put out my hand against him, seeing he is the Lord's anointed."*

That statement wasn't just about Saul, it was about David's own fear of the Lord and his respect for divine authority, even when the vessel was failing.

Let's not romanticize Saul. He was deeply flawed. He started well, but ended in spiritual ruin, consulting witches, disobeying God, and attempting murder. He was insecure, volatile, and spiritually reckless. And yet, he was still the one whom God had anointed. He was still the man who once prophesied, who once led armies to victory, who once had the Spirit of God fall upon him in power. The people even said, "Is Saul also among the prophets?" He had gifting but no inner transformation. He was powerful, but not processed.

David discerned this. He saw that even though Saul had lost his way, he was still God's chosen, until God said otherwise. So David refused to put his hands, words, or mouth against him. He let God deal with Saul, while he focused on keeping his own heart clean.

So I want to admonish you: even if your name is slandered, your motives questioned, or your seat removed, don't let your hands be stained. Let your fruit speak louder than your frustration. And above all, be careful not to speak against someone whom God still calls His anointed. They may have fallen short, but God still picked them. And you honor God, not just by how you worship, but by how you walk through moments like these.

Honor in ministry is not just about what you do publicly, it's about what you say and how you act privately. True honor shows itself when there's tension or offense, and instead of gossiping or venting to others, you choose to speak directly to the one who has offended you. Honor chooses clarity over assumption and confrontation over speculation.

Assumptions can be dangerous. When you fail to go directly to a leader who may have offended you, you open the door to misinterpretation and exaggeration. Most of what you assume may not even be true. Even God, in His all-knowing nature, models this for us. In Genesis 18, before bringing judgment on Sodom and Gomorrah, God says,

*"I will go down and see whether they have done altogether according to the outcry that has come to me. And if not, I will know." —*Genesis 18:21 (ESV)

God doesn't deal in assumption, so neither should we.

Many times, what we think we've heard or sensed from a leader may change when we sit down in humility and have a real conversation. What seemed unbearable from a distance may be understandable up close. But even if after honest engagement the leader continues to act like Saul, jealous, unyielding, or manipulative, don't let offense or frustration dictate your next move. Stay until God says go.

The honorable path is to wait on divine instruction, not public opinion or private frustration. Don't let the whispers of others move you out; let the voice of the Spirit guide your exit. And if God truly calls you to leave, do so without creating confusion or division. Don't gather people with you as you go. That is not a movement, it's a mutiny. If God has called you, He will also give you a people to run with. Let your integrity be defined by what you didn't say as much as by what you did. If others choose to follow you, let it be because they've heard God, not because you painted your former leadership in a poor light.

Consider Absalom in 2 Samuel 15:1–6 (NKJV):

1 In the course of time, Absalom provided himself with a chariot and horses and with fifty men to run ahead of him. 2 He would get up early and stand by the side of the road leading to the city gate. Whenever anyone came with a complaint to be placed before the king for a decision, Absalom would call out to him, "What town are you from?" He would answer, "Your servant is from one of the tribes of Israel." 3 Then Absalom would say to him, "Look, your claims are valid and proper, but there is no representative of the king to hear you." 4 And Absalom would add, "If only I were appointed judge in the land! Then everyone who has a complaint or case could come to me and I would see that they receive justice." 5 Also, whenever anyone approached him to bow down before him, Absalom would reach out his hand, take hold of him and kiss him. 6 Absalom behaved in this way toward all the Israelites who came to the king asking for justice, and so he stole the hearts of the people of Israel.

He stole the hearts of the people through subtle conversations that undermined his father David's leadership. Instead of going directly to David with concerns, he stood at the gate, sympathizing with disgruntled citizens and positioning himself as a better alternative. His dishonor began not with rebellion, but with a tone, a conversation, a whisper. What started as charisma turned into a coup.

What You Sow Is What You'll Fear

Here's the spiritual law: however you leave, you'll always expect others to leave you the same way. If you exit dishonorably, you'll live with the anxiety that someone under you will do the same. That's why some leaders morph into the very thing they once criticized, they become a Saul or an Absalom. Both were emotional leaders, led by their wounds and ego rather than by the Spirit of God.

But David gives us a better model. Even when Saul tried to kill him, David refused to retaliate. He didn't slander or strike. And later, when his own son Absalom rose against him, David again chose to trust God with the outcome rather than fight dirty. David's peace in the chaos came from his posture of honor. He knew that if he had kept his hands clean with Saul, God would keep him covered with Absalom.

To the Emerging Minister: Leave Gently

One of the greatest tests of character in ministry isn't how you enter a place but how you exit it. If you want to be sent off with honor, then you must leave with honor. Leave in such a way that, years from now, you can walk back into that space not to seek reconciliation for damage done, but to be a blessing to the place and the people who helped shape you.

Honor doesn't expire just because your assignment has shifted. If you truly believe your season under a certain leader or church is over, let your departure be marked by respect, not resentment. The goal is not just to leave without offense, but to leave in such a way that the relationship remains intact, even if the structure changes.

Look for ways to intentionally maintain connection with your former leaders. Call them from time to time. Celebrate their birthdays. Publicly honor them whenever possible. Keep them updated on what God is doing in your life not as a report, but as a gesture of respect. These aren't mere formalities; they're acts of honor that remind both you and them that Kingdom family is not disposable. Even if the dynamics have shifted, the foundation of love and respect must remain. Don't slam the door behind you. Close it gently. Leave the hinges oiled with grace so that, if God ever leads you back through it, the door opens freely not with tension or regret.

Breakaways often leave scars in the Body of Christ. But send-offs done with prayer, blessing, and mutual understanding build bridges that outlast seasons. Unfortunately, many ministries have been born from offense, not obedience. Some leaders started churches not because they were sent, but because they were angry, impatient, or nursing a wound. Their pulpits became platforms for their pain instead of places for God's purpose.

Yet, I fully acknowledge: some are truly called out by God to pioneer new works. There are Davids being raised up in the wilderness, not to rebel against Saul, but to lead a new generation in fresh obedience to the Lord. God is still doing a new thing. But when He calls you out, He also calls you to do it right.

Let your fruit be your defense. Let your character speak louder than your calling. And let your exit become as honorable as your entrance. Because in the Kingdom of God, how you leave one place often determines how you will be received in the next.

I am praying that we see fewer breakaways and more Kingdom send-offs.

To Pastors and Church Leaders: Open Your Hands

Now a word to senior leaders: when Jesus gave the Great Commission, He was not relying solely on your church or your ministry. There are people under your care who are being prepared for their own assignments. They are not your property, they are Christ's inheritance. We must remember: it is Christ who died for the Church, and Christ who is building it. And He can raise up anyone He pleases, including someone who is currently serving under you.

When you sense God calling someone to a unique assignment, don't resist release. Be the first to initiate the conversation. Don't wait for it to get awkward. Don't make it hard for them to obey God. Especially when their vision doesn't align with your brand, your network, or your denomination, help them anyway.

Sadly, many leaders only support those starting new works when it's under their umbrella. But when it's something different, something God-breathed but independent, the atmosphere changes. We must grow beyond this territorial spirit. We are all on the same team serving the same Lord. I've seen churches sow financially into those stepping out into new works. That, to me, is beautiful. It's Christlike. And I would love to see more of that spirit in this generation.

In Summary:

Don't assume—investigate with honor.

Don't gossip—go directly.

Don't split—seek to be sent.

Don't manipulate—trust God to assign your tribe.

Don't hold people back—help them launch forward.

Whether you're a young minister preparing to step out or a senior leader helping others rise up, let honor be your guide, not ego, insecurity, or offense.

Kingdom leadership is not about possession, it's about stewardship. And stewardship always ends with release.

Let's build a culture where sons and daughters can rise without rebellion, and fathers and mothers can release without fear.

Made in the USA
Middletown, DE
12 July 2025